HAL•LEONARD
INSTRUMENTAL
PLAY-ALONG

AUDIO
ACCESS
INCLUDED

PLAYBACK+
eed • Pitch • Balance • Loop

# VIOLIN

## THE VERY BEST OF

T0085062

To access audio visit:
**www.halleonard.com/mylibrary**

Enter Code
3134-9025-8855-6947

ISBN 978-1-4950-9084-4

7777 W. BLUEMOUND RD. P.O. BOX 13819 MILWAUKEE, WI 53213

In Australia Contact:
**Hal Leonard Australia Pty. Ltd.**
4 Lentara Court
Cheltenham, Victoria, 3192 Australia
Email: ausadmin@halleonard.com.au

Visit Hal Leonard Online at
**www.halleonard.com**

# ADAGIO
## from OBOE CONCERTO IN F MINOR
### BWV 1059

By JOHANN SEBASTIAN BACH

VIOLIN

# AIR

from ORCHESTRAL SUITE NO. 3
BWV 1068

Violin

By JOHANN SEBASTIAN BACH

# BIST DU BEI MIR

from NOTEBOOK FOR ANNA MAGDALENA BACH
BWV 508

By GOTTFRIED HEINRICH STÖLZEL

VIOLIN

# BOURRÉE IN E MINOR

from SUITE IN E MINOR FOR LUTE
BWV 996

Violin

By JOHANN SEBASTIAN BACH

# INVENTION NO. 4
## BWV 775

VIOLIN

By JOHANN SEBASTIAN BACH

**Moderately**

Harpsichord

# INVENTION NO. 14
## BWV 785

VIOLIN

By JOHANN SEBASTIAN BACH

# JESU, JOY OF MAN'S DESIRING

from CANTATA 147
BWV 147

VIOLIN

By JOHANN SEBASTIAN BACH

# MINUET

from NOTEBOOK FOR ANNA MAGDALENA BACH

BWV Anh. 116

VIOLIN

Composer Unknown

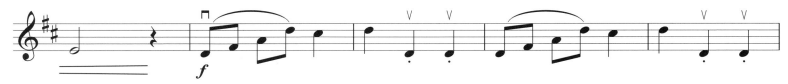

# MINUET IN G MAJOR

from NOTEBOOK FOR ANNA MAGDALENA BACH
BWV Anh. 114

By CHRISTIAN PETZOLD

VIOLIN

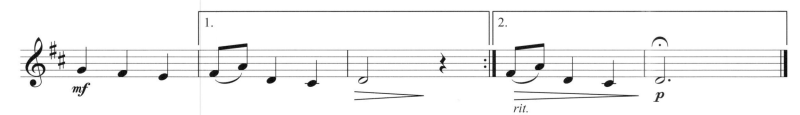

# MINUET IN G MINOR

from NOTEBOOK FOR ANNA MAGDALENA BACH

BWV Anh. 115

By CHRISTIAN PETZOLD

# MUSETTE

from NOTEBOOK FOR ANNA MAGDALENA BACH
BWV Anh. 126

VIOLIN

Composer Unknown

# POLONAISE IN G MINOR

from NOTEBOOK FOR ANNA MAGDALENA BACH
BWV Anh. 119

Composer Unknown

VIOLIN

# SHEEP MAY SAFELY GRAZE

from CANTATA 208
BWV 208

By JOHANN SEBASTIAN BACH

VIOLIN

# SICILIANO
### from FLUTE SONATA IN E-FLAT MAJOR
### BWV 1031

By JOHANN SEBASTIAN BACH

VIOLIN

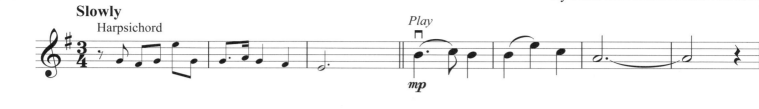

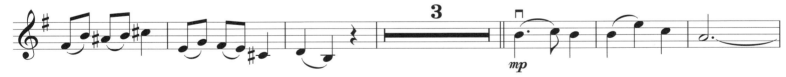

# SLEEPERS, AWAKE
## (Wachet Auf)
from CANTATA 140
BWV 140

By JOHANN SEBASTIAN BACH

VIOLIN